44 Secrets for Great Soccer Goal Scoring Skills

Mirsad Hasic

ISBN: 149239985X
ISBN-13: 978-1492399858

DEDICATION

I dedicate this book all soccer players around the world.

CONTENTS

ACKNOWLEDGMENTS

I would like to thank my family for their support.

1 SHOOTING WITH BOTH LEGS

It wasn't until I started to practice using my left foot that I realized the true power of shooting with both feet.

What's even more surprising is that I now score more goals with my supporting leg than I do with my primary leg.

I'm not talking about using the toe-kick or scoring from one yard after the ball has been crossed inside the 18 yard box.

No, my goals are really amazing, so much so that I still find it hard to believe that I'm actually scoring these incredible goals using my weak foot!

The biggest problem I faced initially – and one that you will likely face too – was teaching my brain to coordinate with the non-primary leg.

For the first few weeks I felt like a novice who was learning stuff from the very beginning. In fact, a novice is exactly what I was with regards to this particular skill.

Honestly, I don't know how many times I got stuck in the ground with my non-primary foot as I attempted to strike the ball.

I remember that first day of practice vividly.

I had so much pain that I had to ice my non-primary foot because it had gotten swollen from hitting the ground so many times.

I won't lie to you and say that this is an easy skill to master because it's not. I actually found it pretty tough to be honest, and I lost count of how many times I wanted to quit because of the slow progress.

However, after few weeks it all started to come together at last. From that moment on, things just went from strength to strength. The key is to keep pushing yourself until you get past that threshold of frustration and discomfort.

If you study professional soccer players you will notice how they are able to score goals with both feet. As soon as an opportunity presents itself, they release the shot without reflecting over which foot they should use.

You see, in professional soccer you have to make decisions fast and seldom have time to set the ball up for your primary foot.

Quite often you will finish an attack with one touch, and that means you must be able to use your non-primary foot with confidence and skill.

If you haven't started to practice shooting with your weaker foot yet, then I suggest you begin immediately. If you don't, you will be wasting valuable time and hindering your progress. The sooner you start, the quicker you will realize the true importance of being able to shoot using both feet.

I can promise you that the hard work and pain you may endure mastering this skill will all seem worth it once you score that first goal with your non-primary foot.

You will get a feeling of jubilation, a sense that the world is your oyster, and nothing or nobody can stop you now! Once you get to experience this for yourself, you will know what I mean.

2 FINISHING IN ONE TOUCH

I don't know how many scoring opportunities I have lost out on during my career by waiting too long to finish the attack, but it must be a lot.

There was a time where I would overanalyze my options once I received the ball.

Needless to say my opponents had little problem clearing the ball away from me because of my dithering.

As I became a more competent player, I learned that finishing as quickly as possible is the secret to scoring more goals.

After implementing this strategy into my game, I was soon able to score more frequently.

I also noticed that the higher the tempo of the game, the faster I needed to finish.

During practice sessions you will obviously have much more time to set the ball up for a scoring opportunity, but during a real competition, the luxury of time is one thing you just don't have.

Any pondering during a serious match will usually result in failure.

Once you receive the ball, or are about to receive it, you must pick the first option that comes into your mind and go with it.

From my experience, the first option is usually the best one anyway, and at least you will attempt to score with it.

This is a much smarter way to play than hesitating; something that is likely to see you lose the ball to opponents and risk a counterattack.

Amateur players who don't regularly get scoring opportunities often hesitate to finish an attack.

This is mainly because they have a hard time deciding which option to go with.

Professional players, on the other hand, never hesitate. They know what the consequences might be if they do.

Although it might look easy when a professional player finishes an attack, you should know that there would have been countless hours of relentless practice gone into his game before he got to play with such skill and dexterity.

My best tip for improving this skill is to start finishing on one touch as you play backyard soccer and during regular practice.

By doing this, you will be gradually changing your mental behavior until it becomes a natural way to play, both in practice and in competition.

I am aware that you will probably miss a lot of shots in the beginning, especially if you're a player who has gotten into the habit of over analyzing your options when a scoring opportunity arises.

But just stick with and don't give up under any circumstances, and you will get better.

I was able to master this skill simply by persevering, so I'm sure you can too!

Obviously I can't say how many extra goals you might score by mastering this tactic because that depends on things like the position you play at; what your current skills are, and the competition you are playing in, etc.

But I can guarantee that as you become more comfortable finishing in one touch, you will certainly get some amazing results because of it.

It's worth mentioning here that finishing in one-touch is one of the more difficult skills to master in soccer.

The reason for this is because it requires great accuracy, good ball technique, and sharp mental focus.

To summarize this chapter: If you really want to become a professional, then finishing in one touch is a skill that you have to get good at, period.

3 HAVING A PLAN FOR SCORING

Trying to score a goal the moment you receive the ball might work in amateur soccer, but in professional competitions things are not that easy.

A professional player needs to know exactly what he will do with the ball even before he receives it.

The concept is a simple one, and that is to ensure you are always one step ahead of your opponents.

During my early years of playing soccer, I often liked to receive the ball, set it up nicely, and then finish the attack.

This worked pretty well most of the time as the competition was generally mediocre at best.

However, as I advanced and began to face more skillful opponents, I soon came to realize that this strategy won't work anymore.

Unlike in the past, rival players were catching up to me the moment I received the ball.

My goal scoring spirit diminished with every failed attempt to set up the ball in preparation for a strike.

It got to the point where I began to pass the ball on to a teammate just because of my inability to plan and execute my scoring attempts quickly, and the subsequent fear of repeated failure.

I knew I needed to do something about this, and fast, so I went to the coach for advice.

He told me I would score a lot more goals if I knew what to do before receiving the ball.

He explained that a skillful player always has a plan of action, and without one, the chances of scoring are greatly reduced.

In the game that followed I decided to follow the coach's advice and put his suggested method to the test, or at least have a go.

However, changing my mental behavior proved to be much tougher than I thought it would.

I had become so comfortable with receiving the ball, setting it up, and then releasing the shot, that this had become my natural way of playing.

Now I had to think in a whole new way, and immediately know what to do with the ball as I got it. This was the complete opposite of what I had become used to.

I believe it took me an entire season before I eventually got to grasp this new approach, but I go there in the end, and what a difference it made to my game.

I noticed how my finishing had a much better accuracy rate compared to how it was previously.

Because you are reading this book, I know that you are also keen to continuously work on improving your skills.

Therefore, I suggest you start getting into the habit of planning your moves before receiving the ball.

By having a plan of action and the ability to execute it successfully, means you get to stand out from the crowd as your performance becomes more and more successful on the field.

Remember, forward-thinking is not a guarantee for goal scoring.

As I said previously, this depends on other factors too, like the level of competition, your own skills, making the right decisions and so on.

However, it will definitely improve your scoring statistics.

Even if you only score one or two extras goals every now and again, it is still worth managing this skill.

4 DON'T STAND

A player who is constantly on the move is twice as hard to mark as one who is standing still and just hoping that the ball will find its way to his feet.

While this is a simple tactic, I will be first to admit that I frequently forget to move during games in my early days as a player.

As soon as you start to move more, and continue moving, you will get to realize how you're better able to create more scoring opportunities for both you and your teammates.

Movement also helps to disorientate the opponents, and any way to sidetrack the opposition can only be a good thing.

This approach obviously requires good stamina, and that means you will need to be as fit as a butcher's dog and well trained too.

The secret here is to move wisely and not just run around for the sake of it.

The last thing you want to do is exhaust all your energy and not be able to pick up the pace when you need to most.

OK, so let's look at how you can tell when you should move and when you should conserve energy.

From my own personal experience I have always found it best to start moving as soon as the ball is around me.

I usually begin by taking off in different directions so as to make it difficult for the opponent to mark me.

I do everything I can to confuse and distract him from the ball.

Opponents often used to tell me that I was a pain to mark because I was never still.

Some even said they were glad when the game was over because they were absolutely exhausted just trying to keep up and cover me.

Others confessed that they probably couldn't have gone on for much longer.

You may end up running around a lot and not even get to have the ball, but I can assure you that it will pay off sooner or later.

You just need to have patience and always be prepared for those scoring opportunities as and when they arise.

On the other hand, if you just stand around on the field like some statuette, then you will never get to score, especially against strong opponents.

If you want a clear example of a player who never stood still, just take a look at Filippo Inzaghi who played for A.C Milan.

Commentators often referred to him as the guy who must have been born offside because of his stamina to keep constantly on the move.

Inzaghi often scored goals from out of nowhere and everywhere; the main reason being that he was never still and always around when opportunities occurred.

You would see him chasing the ball around the pitch like a ravenous tiger!

It will pay you to embrace a similar approach if you are going to score goals.

Try to be constantly mindful on the importance of moving on the field, especially when it matters most.

The only time where standing works as a tactic is when you play backyard soccer with your friends.

In real competition, against real opponents, you will never score by being still.

So remember to move no matter what, even if you don't get a single scoring opportunity during the entire game, just keep on moving.

5 POWERLESS SHOT

When inexperienced players find themselves inside the 18 yard box, they often fire the hardest possible shot they can muster and just hope for the best.

Experienced goal scorers follow a different strategy. They rarely shoot using a full-force kick unless a situation warrants it.

Instead, they send the ball with more accuracy and less power.

When I was a less experienced player, whenever the ball was near me inside the 18 yard box, I would boot it with all the power I could conjure up.

Once the kick was released, all I could do was cross my fingers and hope for a good outcome.

Such shots were a total failure more often than not.

At the moment of strike, I usually had my head buried into the ground with teeth gritted and no real focus or control as to what had just happened.

This slapdash approach would result in either a missed shot or one that would go directly to the keeper, thus enabling him to block or catch the ball with relative ease.

If you study professional players and their finishing, you will notice how they rarely shoot with full power unless the situation justifies it.

When you monitor them carefully, you can see that they shoot with proportional power and great aim, and certainly out of the keeper's reach.

This is something I had never realized until I started to play alongside the top scorer of our league.

During a training session one day, as we were aiming shots at the keeper, this guy asked me why I was shooting with my instep (arched middle part of the foot between the toes and the ankle) all the time.

I told him that this works best for me because I can generate the most power on the ball, which obviously increases my chances of scoring.

He looked at me quizzically and said:

"Mirsad, most of my goals are scored by using the inside of my foot. I will hopefully be able to show you later today what I mean by that."

Somewhere around the middle of the first half he found himself just outside the 18 yard box with a perfect shooting opportunity.

Instead of charging and releasing a powerful shot, as I would have done, he simply aimed at the top right corner of the goal and made a pretty low-powered shot using the inside part of his foot.

The ball traveled through the air with an element of majesty and well out of the keeper's reach. It was the perfect goal!

After the game he came over and asked if I had noticed how he scored.

I said that I had, and that would never have believed it before today.

He suggested I stop my full-powered approach when shooting near the 18 yard box, and proposed I try his method for the next few games instead.

I agreed to give it a go, and was now eager to experiment using the inside of my foot.

During the next game I got a goal scoring opportunity.

Remembering what I had been told, I attempted to aim perfectly as I fired my first shot with limited power using the inside of the foot.

Amazingly, the keeper failed to dive quickly enough and the ball suddenly found its way to the back of the net.

I couldn't believe what had just happened, and for a few moments wasn't even aware that I had actually scored.

From that moment on, I never used my instep to strike the ball again when in the area of the 18 yard box.

My rule of thumb was to now only fire powerful shots with the instep when I was more than five yards outside the penalty box.

If you're making the mistakes that I was, then I suggest you try this approach too.

This tactic has worked wonders for my goal scoring skills, and I'm sure it will do exactly the same for yours too.

6 KEEPER'S POSITION

One of the most noticeable differences between a true goal scorer and a player who rarely scores is that the skilled one always checks the position of the keeper before taking his shot.

He actually follows the goalie's movements even when he's 40 yards from the goalmouth.

The reason why he monitors the keeper's position is because it enables him to surprise the goalie if he is too far away from his goal line.

A goalkeeper is at his most vulnerable when he's not expecting a shot, which is something experienced players love to take advantage of.

I'm not saying that you should take every opportunity to fire a long-range shot at the opponent's goal.

You need to carefully evaluate your options and decide whether the keeper is far away enough from his goal to justify such a kick.

And even if you think he is, you still need to decide whether there's a reasonable chance of beating him or not from where you are positioned.

Some years ago, I actually managed to score a goal directly from the kick off.

I saw the opportunity when the keeper was standing at the 18 yard box waiting for the game to begin.

As my teammate passed the ball to me, I quickly received it and crossed it over the keeper's head as he remained on the same spot as kick off.

His face was a picture!

The poor guy just stood there motionless, completely confused as to what had just happened.

I've noticed how goalkeepers often stand a few yards from the goal line in order to cut off the angles. They also do this to make themselves look bigger.

If you think about it, a goalkeeper looks pretty small when he is standing at the goal line, but as he moves few yards away from it, he suddenly appears bigger.

Goalkeepers are no different to the outside players in that they also have their vulnerabilities and make mistakes.

Getting to know the opposition's goalie allows you to take advantage of his shortcomings.

An amateur will often forget to move back to the goal line as the ball approaches the 18 yard box, and that is something which gives you an ideal scoring opportunity.

As I mentioned previously, I managed to score a goal from the kick off, but I've also played with those who were able to score from 60 yards.

This was possible for no other reason than the keepers were standing too far from their goal lines at the time, and they didn't realize the danger until it was too late.

However, don't expect to score on every occasion where an opportunity presents itself.

You really do need to be able to fire a long range shot with great accuracy, while at the same time release the ball with enough power to reach the opponent's goal.

To summarize this chapter: I want you to remember that the key with this skill is to carefully monitor the keeper without being too obvious.

Before taking a shot, you need to decide whether there is a reasonable chance of scoring or whether the goalkeeper is perhaps too close to the goal line. If in doubt, don't go for it!

7 OVER ANALYZING

One of the biggest pitfalls when it comes to scoring goals is that of over-analyzing situations and thinking far too much about possible options.

Many amateurs will approach the keeper and start wondering whether they should dribble him, or what side to aim for, should they pass the ball to a teammate, and whatever else might come to mind at the time.

Players who think too much often miss out on a lot of scoring opportunities.

Just know that to overanalyze is a hindrance to you and your team, not a help.

The consequence of thinking too much is that you end up dithering when you should be taking fast, decisive action.

If you have ever listened to professional soccer players in interviews, the one thing they all say is that it's never a good idea to overanalyze any situation.

Basically, any player who overanalyzes is lacking somewhat in his confidence, and questioning his own ability.

The best way to get over this is to simply get on with things.

Just fire that ball in the direction of the goal with same confidence as you have when kicking a ball around with your friends in the backyard.

This method might sound a bit too simplistic, but really it's not.

The right approach in soccer is as much to do with having the correct mindset as it is having the physical capability, especially when it comes to scoring goals.

In order to score goals you should not overthink your options too much.

Instead, just focus on getting that ball past the goal line.

I know this might sound too simplistic, but the fact is this: the more you think about stuff the more you'll overcomplicate things, and once that happens, your momentum is lost.

Let's look at how you might apply this simplistic approach to your game.

Say you are approaching the goalkeeper in a one-on-one duel. Here you should pick the "first" option that pops up in your mind and forget about the rest.

Don't change your decision or allow doubt to creep in. If you do, there's a good chance you will lose the opportunity to score.

I must confess that I tended to overanalyze scoring opportunities before I became a more experienced player.

I never understood how bad this was until one day the coach asked me if I thought I was over-thinking my options whenever I had the ball at my feet.

I was not really sure what the man meant by this at the time. I was certainly curious to know what he thought he saw in my game that I didn't, so I asked him to elaborate.

He explained that thinking too much about what options are available can have a negative impact on the way someone plays.

He then went on to say that he'd noticed my hesitancy whenever I was presented with a goal scoring opportunity. 'Analysis paralysis' he called it.

So he asked me again, am I trying to weigh up my options before striking the ball?

I told him that this was exactly what I do, thinking it was wise to weight up ones options before making the final kick.

He said that this approach is anything but wise, especially in competitive soccer.

The coach explained that the only way I would get to score more goals would be to break the habit of over-thinking.

He said I should go with the first option that comes into my head and follow through with it, and if any other thoughts come up, I need to just discard them and press on with option one.

The advice I got on that day from that particular coach was a game changer for me.

From that moment on, I began to score twice as many goals as I did when I would over-analyze situations.

This was not a hard habit to break either, and with every goal scored, my new way of thinking was reinforced still further, until it eventually became natural to me.

To summarize this chapter: Even though you need to have good physical skills with the ball in order to score goals, you also need to have the right mental approach.

Any old thinking pattern that gets in the way of your game has to go, especially one of over-analysis.

It doesn't matter how powerful, controlled, or accurate your shooting is, if you are over-thinking your options during a competition, then you are losing out on crucial goal scoring opportunities.

8 FIRST ON THE BALL

The player who is first on the ball is usually the one who wins the duel.

If you want to score goals then you will need to be first on the ball once it's crossed inside the 18 yard box.

The moment you are inside the 18 yard box, your mission is to score, plain and simple!

Obviously you opponents will do everything they can to prevent you from reaching the ball first.

At times, this might include unfair treatment such as pulling on your shirt or shoving you on the back.

I've experienced this kind of behavior a lot in my time, and as irritating as it is, this just the way things are out there on the field during a competitive match.

Being first on the ball will often result in you having to sacrifice yourself.

That means there will be times where a race to it will hurt, but if you want to score goals, then you need to understand that pain is all par for the course.

Quite often, and out of desperation, opponents will do everything in their power to stop you.

They care little whether you get hurt or not, so long as you don't score.

So just how do you reach the ball first without causing a foul by using unfair treatment like some players do?

The best approach is that of belief.

You have to really and truly believe that you can be first on the ball and not just "try" to be first. Seriously, mindset plays a huge role in fast moving soccer.

The mental aspect of this approach cannot be emphasized strongly enough.

How you think can influence how you act, and how you act determines the outcome of a given situation, i.e. its success of failure.

As you start to study professional soccer players, you will notice one thing that they all have in common, and that is their determination to reach the ball first.

Look carefully and you can really see in their eyes that they have convinced themselves that it is they who will be first on the ball.

I can assure you that any player who utilizes this skill efficiently becomes far better at scoring compared to someone with good skills yet an inability to be first on the ball.

Having good ball control skills is not worth very much if you don't have the ball!

I've played with guys who were not all that good when it came to dribbling past defenders, yet they scored countless goals for no other reason than their ability to reach the ball first.

To summarize this chapter: You must have that "eye of the tiger" look about you, and a genuine belief that you can be first on the ball and score more goals.

If you can embrace this mindset, this behavior, then I guarantee you will notice some really great results when it comes to goal scoring.

9 FOLLOWING UP IN THE ATTACK

In order to score goals you have to follow up in every single attack, even if you don't get a single scoring opportunity during the whole game.

Being far from the ball will not transform you into a goal scorer; a misguided concept too many players like to believe!

I know this firsthand because I used to be one of these delusional players.

I would often be far away from the ball yet complained how I rarely got the chance to score.

The reason I was so frequently distanced from the ball was because of my reluctance to follow up in an attack.

I understand that now!

So always make sure you follow up with every attack, even when you think the chances of getting your feet on the ball are minimal.

In soccer, you never quite know which way the ball will take off, and suddenly you can be presented with a scoring opportunity because of an unexpected rebound, for example.

Something you must never do is become disappointed if you rarely receive the ball, or when you don't seem to get too many goal scoring opportunities.

There may be times where you feel as though all the hard work and sacrifice that you've put into your game is not rewarding you for your efforts, but take heed!

Such an attitude will drag you down, and might even see you quit if you let it fester for long enough.

Just be mindful of the fact that this game is all about patience and persistence, and those who work through both the good, and not so good times, are the ones who always win through in the end.

I constantly encourage myself to keep working at improving my game, especially during those times where things don't seem to be working out in my favor.

I do this by telling myself that the opportunities will come sooner or later, providing I keep striving for them.

I've scored several goals without expecting to, simply by following up in all attacks whether I thought it was a good idea at the time or not.

If you are someone who has been struggling to score your first goal despite your best efforts, then you might have a hard time believing what I write here.

Please just trust me on this one.

Keep working at your game and never give up because of setbacks.

There are many barriers to overcome in soccer, some easy, others more difficult, but the only way to climb over each one is to never give in.

Once you get over a hurdle there is no looking back, and the rewards are well worth the efforts.

Hard work always pays off in the end, and once any new achievement has been accomplished, it is then easier to motivate yourself to work even harder, with renewed vigor, and even more determination than before.

This approach will see you become the best that you can be.

Another good reason why you should always try to follow up in an attack is because it will force the opponents to mark you.

Because of this, you will be indirectly creating more scoring opportunities for your teammates.

10 OVERDOING SCORING

There was a time when I was really good at overdoing things on the pitch.

Whenever I had a great scoring opportunity, I would regularly lose out because of my inability to finish the attack.

After successfully dribbling an opponent, I would often have a clear chance to score, but instead I would wait for another challenger to approach and attempt to dribble him as well.

I would continue dribbling until I'd eventually lose the ball, or if I didn't get dribbled twice, I would try to set up the ball perfectly in preparation for the final attack.

This also resulted in more lost goal scoring opportunities than I care to remember.

You see, my dithering would allow time for an opponent to close in, and that meant he was now so close that a shot was no longer possible.

It was certainly hard work being me back in the day, that's for sure!

It wasn't unusual for the coach to get so mad that he would place me on the bench.

He warned me time and time again to stop playing like this, but I continued as if I were hardwired to perform this way and completely unable to change.

He told the team one day that he realized I was too good to be sitting on the bench, but because of my arrogant attitude and reluctance to change, he had no choice but to put me there.

On that note, he then announced that there was a seat reserved for me on the bench for the foreseeable future.

So that was it, his decision had been made.

I spent several games on that bench and it was just awful. I eventually came to realize that I would need to stop overdoing my scoring opportunities.

I would also have to change my attitude and stop playing with such arrogance if I were to get another chance to play a full game.

This episode had seen me eat humble pie alright, but looking back, it was exactly what I needed at the time.

The next time I was allowed to play, the coach warned me that if I start to overdo things again he would not hesitate to put me back on the bench.

This humiliation had proved to be a great lesson for me personally. From that moment on I started to finish the scoring opportunities as soon as I got past the challenger.

Not only did the games become more enjoyable (much to my surprise), but I was suddenly scoring a lot more goals.

In fact, I became one of the top scorers in our team, and we also got into the Team of the Month for our competition.

I got moved to the senior team that year because of my continuity of play and enhanced performance on the field.

My coach also pointed out that a positive change in attitude had played a big part in my promotion too.

He said that if I hadn't changed my behavior then he would have recommended another player for the senior team.

The lessons I took from all of this was that I may never have made the senior team if I had continued to overdo scoring opportunities and refused to listen to the advice of others more experienced than me.

Furthermore, if I had continued with the "I know best" attitude, then I would not have scored as many goals as I did do; goals, I hasten to add, that helped lead our team to victories.

And at the end of the day, winning is the most important thing when competing on the soccer field.

If you are a player who tends to overdo scoring opportunities, and maybe even play with a little arrogance, then I suggest you do everything you can to stop this behavior right now.

The time has come to readjust your approach, not only for yourself, but also for the benefit of your team.

Sometimes we can't see ourselves how others see us. Just because you think your way of doing things is right, that doesn't always mean it is.

It just means you think it is!

Listen to those with more experience than you, be willing to eat a little humble pie if necessary, and prepare to change for the better.

You'll be glad you did!

11 SAVE ENERGY

If you wear yourself out early on and become completely exhausted by half time, then you can't expect to perform at your best for the whole match.

Imagine setting up the ball for a scoring opportunity when you're absolutely drained.

Understandably, you chances of succeeding are going to be greatly diminished.

Quite often, you will get an ideal scoring opportunity after completing a run of 20-30 yards, but for that you need oomph and plenty of it too!

This solution therefore is to conserve energy when there's a chance to do so.

This way you will have the power to perform when you most need it.

Soccer is a game that has to have momentum from start to finish, and players need to be able to fire well-aimed shots with sufficient power in order to beat the opponents' keeper.

A team that is able to maintain its performance throughout the game is a team that has learned to conserve its energy properly.

I made the mistake of burning up all my energy a lot in the past, usually far too early in the game and quite unnecessarily.

This was usually done by chasing and marking opponents that my teammates were supposed to cover.

Then, if and when I finally got a chance to score, I would be way too exhausted to perform with any real success.

Knowing how to save your energy is all about balance.

Helping your team and helping your teammates are two different things, and it's important to distinguish between them.

Helping your team is all about doing what is required of you to the best of your ability. Each player has his own duties and should stick closely to them.

When you start covering what another team player is supposed to be doing, as well as your own tasks, is when you start wasting valuable energy.

When you learn to conserve energy effectively you will be able to score more goals. It really is as simple as that.

The more energy you have, the more physically and mentally charged you will be, and that means you're better able to execute shots at the goal with drive and enthusiasm.

Being sapped of all energy, on the other hand, has the total opposite effect.

Once I stopped doing the work of others, I had so much more energy during the games.

Needless to say that whenever scoring opportunities presented themselves I was now able to do something useful with the ball, unlike before where I barely had enough power to pick it up, let alone kick it!

Not managing energy efficiently is one of the biggest mistakes amateur players make.

Because of their inexperience, they are not always able to decide when and where to use their valuable energy resources to the best advantage.

Obviously a good soccer player needs to be incredibly fit, and he also has to have stamina too, if he's to be useful from start to finish.

If you think your game is not as good as it might be, and you find it a real hard slog to keep going for the entire match, then think on.

This might be for no other reason than you're not making smart choices with regards to conserving energy.

Hopefully this chapter will get you thinking about maintaining energy levels, and persuade you to examine the way you play in more detail.

12 DON'T UNDERESTIMATE THE TOE KICK

A lot of players want to make their scoring attempts look as spectacular as possible by choosing the right option for finishing an attack.

Some believe that trying to score with the toe-kick is a rookie approach and would make them look unprofessional.

This is why so few players include this as a goal scoring option.

I can tell right away that treating the toe kick as some kind of rookie shot is complete hogwash.

This has been one of my best weapons when it comes to scoring goals.

The toe kick is especially useful when you are inside the 18 yard box surrounded by several opponents.

In cases like this, there's just no time to set the ball up for a controlled shot.

The best thing about the toe kick is that you can actually get a really powerful strike on the ball, even when you are standing completely still.

Professionals use it all the time, and if it's good enough for them, then it's worth using as part of your own scoring strategy too.

This is not to say there are no disadvantages with the toe-kick because there are.

Perhaps the biggest one is that it's quite difficult to aim and control the shot.

At its worst, it can be highly unpredictable, which means the ball may fail to reach its target.

It might also prove embarrassing, depending just how far off course the ball actually goes.

There is also the risk of getting hurt if you don't strike the ball properly.

But all in all, the toe-kick is a valuable option when conditions call for it.

The sheer joy of seeing that ball fly past the goal line and into the net from a powerful toe kick is priceless.

I've played with guys over the years that blatantly refused to exploit the toe kick because they believed it was something that only toddlers and beginners use.

Refusing to use this method of kicking out of embarrassment, or some false belief, is their loss.

Their ignorance is also a gain for any rival team they to play that happily employs the toe-kick into their strategy.

To give you an example of how efficient the toe kick actually is, I would like you to study my personal role model, who also happens to be one of the, if not the, greatest goal scorers ever to be: Mr. Ronaldo Luís Nazário de Lima.

If you study his goal scoring carefully, you will see how he'd often finish with a toe kick.

He would frequently find himself surrounded by several opponents and just didn't have the time to set up the ball for a more controlled finish.

Ronaldo was a true goal-scoring machine and he only cared about getting that ball past the keeper and into the back of the net.

He didn't worry about how he scored his goals, nor did he care about impressing others with fancy shots.

His only focus was to score using whatever method was available at the time.

Ronaldo was indisputably one of the greatest players ever to have used the toe-kick for scoring multiple goals throughout his career. Surely then, you ought to be using it too as and when the time warrants?

If you can get past the fact that a toe kick doesn't look fancy, but then accept the fact that it can be a highly effective way for scoring more goals, then you too will be able to score additional goals during your own soccer career.

13 BEING SELFISH AND SELFLESS

A smart goal scorer is one who is able to decide wisely when it's right to be selfish and finish an attack himself, or when he should pass the ball over to a better positioned teammate.

Your desire to score goals can easily overwhelm your number one priority on the field, which is to always play for the team first and not for your own glory.

Most of us have come across selfish, self-centered, self-seeking players at some point, and if you haven't, I will just add "yet" to that statement.

I can recall playing with a teammate some years back who was perhaps the most egocentric player I had ever come across, and I don't think I've met anyone quite as bad as him since.

He simply didn't care whether another teammate was better placed than him or not.

All he cared about was whether he could score himself so that he could revel in his own glory.

He would often shoot the moment he got the ball; even if he happened to be 40 yards away from the goal!

The flip side of this guy was another teammate who never actually finished an attack despite having completely open goals on many occasions.

He would always try to find someone else to pass the scoring opportunity to. I remember one time where he even stopped the ball on the goal line and played it backwards!

As you can see, whether you are too selfish or completely selfless, it's not always easy to get the right balance.

I can assure you there will be occasions where you get to hear people telling you you're selfish, even if your intentions and decisions are the right ones for a given situation.

This is something you just can't avoid hearing if you want to score goals at a regular basis.

As long as you know you're not intentionally selfish and thinking only about your own glory, then you will be fine.

Providing you always try to do the right thing, then any moans from other players that lose out on scoring opportunities will be minimal.

However, if you are aware that there are times where you perhaps should have passed the ball to a better positioned teammate, but didn't, because you wanted to finish in order to feed your own ego, then it really is time to step back and reassess your approach, especially if you missed some or all of those goals.

In order to score plenty of goals though, you do need to be a little bit selfish, so long as it's not to the extreme.

Giving up a goal scoring opportunity to another, better positioned player, takes a bit of getting used to, particularly in a situation where you could still score yourself, albeit the chance is less than if you pass the ball over another player.

Judging the conditions is something that requires a lot of game experience, and that can only come from playing in lots of competitions.

It also requires you to continuously assesses and reassess your game as you progress.

Thinking back, it probably took me several years to really develop this skill.

Or certainly to the level where I was able to decide whether I should try to score or pass the ball to a better placed teammate.

Sometimes there is no clear-cut answer of when to be selfish and when to be selfless because each and every situation on a soccer field is unique.

To summarize this chapter: I would say that the best method for developing your decision making is to always take the common sense approach.

Try to pick the option you believe is in the best interest of the team as a whole.

Get into the habit of being mindful of each situation you encounter.

Do this, and you will begin to balance fairly between selfish and unselfish behavior on the pitch.

14 BEATING YOUR FEAR FOR MISSING

I remember when I first started to play soccer.

I must have been the worst player ever when it came to finishing a scoring opportunity, or at least it felt that way at the time.

Whenever the ball was crossed from the side, I always managed to either hit the posts or send the ball flying over the goal.

My teammates were supportive and always encouraged me to keep working at my scoring, despite the fact that I was lousy at it.

In fact, I was worse than useless because I would frequently miss open goals too.

It was pointed out to me by the coach one day that FEAR was hindering my attempts, but fear of what, I had no idea!

Even to this day I find it unbelievable how I missed so many scoring chances, especially the open goals.

After all, the only requirement was to send the ball into the right direction.

Yet the more I missed, the worse I got, and it was getting me down big time.

When it became obvious to all those around me that I was getting nowhere fast, the coach took me aside and explained my problem with more clarity than he had done previously.

He said that each failed attempt was reinforcing a fear of failure within me, and so I had to change my way of thinking if I were to ever get over this dilemma.

He even had a name for it: "Atychiphobia." An abbreviation I like to reflect on when it came to my panic on the pitch is one where FEAR stands for: False Experiences Appearing Real

So now that the problem had been property identified, a solution could be sought.

But because this fear of failure had gone on for so long, it was to take me a good while to get over it.

I got there eventually though, thanks to the support and encouragement of my teammates.

My approach was to practice on nothing more than getting that ball past the goal line.

I used as much concentration as I could muster to focus on the task.

This exercise gradually reversed my belief mechanism. So now, each time I got the ball into the goal, that successful attempt was mentally reinforced.

So with each successful goal, I was banking yet another accomplishment into my psyche.

The more I banked, the more confident I became with my ability to score, and less fearful of failure. In other words, assurance was replacing fear.

Players that miss simple goal scoring opportunities, more often or not, are probably suffering with a fear of failure as I was, rather than a lack of actual ability.

This is a cycle that will never break unless they identify their problem and work on the solution.

The brain is a powerful organ and can affect us in both positive and negative ways.

The good news is that the mind can be trained to behave as we wish it to.

Overconfidence can be as much a hindrance as underconfidence, so the key in any situation it to be realistic and accept what is true.

Once that's been established, we can then give the brain exercises to reinforce the correct beliefs.

If you want to become something more than just a Joe Average player, then you need to develop the right attitude, beliefs, and a healthy mindset.

To summarize this chapter: Train your brain! Overcome any fear of failure you may have by using reverse psychology.

15 REMAINING CALM IN ONE-ON-ONE DUELS

The ability to remain calm in stressful situations is one of the skills that separate true goal scoring machines with players who never, or rarely, get to score in spite of their best efforts.

In order to develop this skill you will need to be confident in your ability, and truly believe that you are capable of beating the keeper.

If you watch professional players on TV, as they face the keeper in a one-on-one duel, you will notice how calm they appear to be.

They also make everything look effortless as they put the ball away.

In many cases, when a keeper is challenged by a competent and confident player, he becomes downright defenseless.

Don't be fooled by the apparent ease in which a professional player wins these duels.

Just because it looks easy, that doesn't mean it is of course, it just means it looks that way.

Making something difficult look effortless is the mark of a true professional.

Obviously a qualified player has not got to where he is by coincidence.

Just like you and me they have to work hard at improving and maintaining their game.

You can learn an awful lot from studying the experts though, especially their body language.

When facing a keeper in a one-on-one duel, this is as much a challenge of the minds as it is of the body.

From my own experience, I have learned that it's really important to wait for the keeper to make the first move in a duel, e.g., diving for the ball.

In most cases he will be aggressive in his approach and try to make himself look big.

If you can remain calm throughout the challenge, then the chance of scoring is in your favor.

I once played with a striker who did everything right on the field and really played a good game...until he approached the goal area with the ball!

It was frustrating to watch him go to pieces in these situations. He often failed to finish the scoring opportunity by choosing the most insane option he could think of.

His problem was not a lack of talent, but his seeming inability to remain calm when confronted.

He frequently missed out on scoring chances by this constant blundering every time he was anywhere near the goal.

What was so frustrating is that he was actually a very precise and disciplined goal scorer - from a distance!

Yet the moment he was faced with a one-on-one duel with a keeper he would completely break down.

I once asked him why he always lost his nerve whenever he was challenged by the goalie.

He just said that he couldn't remain calm in challenging situations like this as he felt immensely intimidated.

He went on to say that when he approaches a goalkeeper, he can't help but visualize him as some kind of threatening species who is impossible to beat.

"When the panic sets in is when I usually opt for the most ridiculous move," he said. *"I just want to clear the ball away and get out of the keeper's territory as quickly as I possibly can."*

This was yet another case of mind over matter. The more he feared a one-on-one duel with the goalie, the more he reinforced this dread of his into his psyche.

When left untreated, this way of thinking has a real potential to eventually stop a player entering the goalkeeping area altogether.

The only way players like this can overcome their fears, is to reverse the way they think about things and just find a way past the goalie.

That's it!

Once again, with the proper training, support from the team, and some positive reinforcement, it is very possible to change the thinking pattern.

The player in this example can get to challenge goalkeepers with renewed vigor and a fresh enthusiasm, providing of course, he is willing to change.

To summarize this chapter with a quote:

"When you change the way you look at things, the things you look at change."

16 HIDING YOURSELF

One of the biggest mistakes you can make in soccer is to hide yourself on the field and never take that final step to see an attack through.

It's obviously impossible to get a goal if you are hiding away every time a scoring opportunity presents itself, yet many players do just that!

Looking back, I used to do this a fair bit in my early career, but I was oblivious to it at the time.

I just could not figure out why I wasn't scoring goals.

I thought there was something wrong with the way I played, which there was of course, but it wasn't my inability to play soccer, but my reluctance to step up to the challenge when opportunities arose.

So it was my mindset, and not a physical inability, that was getting in the way here.

During one of our games, the coach took me to one side and asked why I stepped away every time a scoring opportunity landed at my feet.

He said I displayed awesome shooting and finishing skills at the practice sessions, so why wasn't I making use of them during actual competitions?

It's strange how others can see things in you that you can't always see in yourself.

Of course the coach was right.

His words changed something within me and I suddenly felt a new sense of enthusiasm.

I was now more than willing to get back out there and start with a fresh new approach.

Now that I knew what the problem was, the solution was evident.

I simply had to change the way I played to match that of the practice sessions.

It wasn't too long before I lost my inhibitions in competition and began scoring some great goals.

The art of scoring goals has a lot to do with challenging any negative mental behaviors and turning them around towards a more positive way of thinking.

Sometimes the switch can be made by someone pointing something out to you that you were unaware of yourself, as was the case with me.

Other times, it might be a negativity that is hardwired into your way of thinking.

In cases such as that it will require more work to alter the mindset, but it can still be done, it just takes a little longer, that's all.

Adopting a positive mindset and having clear objectives is a great way to stand out from the pack.

The way you feel drastically influences the way you play soccer. Therefore, having the right attitude, and with no inhibitions, could be your ticket to higher competition, and even see a professional contract come your way.

One of my teammates actually signed up for a professional club after he scored over 20 goals for our team in a single season.

To be honest, he was not what you might call exceptional, but he showed promise, determination, and was always open to constructive criticism and suggestions.

He also took responsibility to finish an attack in every instance, and perhaps most importantly, he was never afraid to fail.

"The only real failure in life is the failure to try." ~ *George Bernard Shaw*

If you recognize yourself as someone who often shies away from scoring opportunities, then you will need to address this behavior and begin to turn it around to one which is more positive and bold.

To score goals you need to show yourself, scream for the ball, and have the confidence and determination to follow through with the finish.

If you don't, then the chances of never or rarely scoring are high.

It's my guess you don't want that since you have read down this far into the book.

17 PRESSING THE KEEPER

A lot of goalies actually have poor ball handling skills, namely dribbling, passing, or receiving the ball.

This is especially the case with those that have never competed as an outfield player.

What this means is that they will often feel insecure once the ball is passed over to them.

Their uneasy behavior is pretty simple to spot.

It's also a great opportunity for you to exploit their vulnerability and place them under pressure once they have the ball.

Some professional keepers are so poor at handling the ball with their feet that they clear it away the second it reaches them.

When you spot a goalie clearing the ball with a degree of panic, or looking generally nervous about touching it with his feet, this is your cue to act.

Keepers, like all other players, will make most of their mistakes when they are put under a lot of pressure.

It is your job to apply this pressure, and if you can get the goalie into a flap, then your chance of scoring is increased greatly.

The key to succeeding with this strategy is to think fast and attack the moment an opportunity presents itself.

I'm sure you must have seen players go in to attack a goalkeeper as he prepares to clear the ball away.

In occurrences like these, it's not unusual for the goalie to actually hit the player with the ball.

These situations obviously create great scoring opportunities.

During a cup final once, we were facing a team that had really good players.

Nevertheless, it wasn't too long before I noticed how their keeper had real problems controlling the ball with his feet.

This was particularly obvious when he got backward passes as he mostly cleared the ball into throw-ins.

During one situation, where I was pretty close to the opponent's goal, I saw that the one of the defenders was about to pass the ball to the keeper.

The moment he passed it across, I rushed in right away putting the goalie under immediate pressure.

I also jumped into the path of the ball, and as the goalie attempted to clear it, the ball rebounded off my back and sprung right into the goal.

We won the game, and that was one of the easiest goals I'd ever scored.

Most goals are scored with the feet or the head, but to get one in off the back is certainly one to remember!

To summarize this chapter: You should not run on every ball that is played backwards to the keeper.

Instead, pick your runs wisely and try to use them to place the goalie under pressure.

Remember, this tactic works best against goalkeepers who have weak ball handling skills, so be on the lookout for those guys.

18 RECEIVING THE BALL AT SPEED

Receiving the ball while running at a fast pace, and close to the goal, puts you in a very advantageous position.

In this situation, the chance of scoring is much higher compared to one where you are motionless.

Additionally, your opponents will have a much harder job catching up with you when you're on the move, and this gives you a few yards lead on them.

A lot of amateur players give this little consideration. Instead, they just stand around in one spot waiting for the ball to find its way over to their feet.

Such an approach might work in amateur soccer, but if you want to play professionally then you have to be on your toes.

That means you have to have your running feet ready at all times, prepared to sprint off at a moment's notice.

The best approach is to be in movement as the ball comes towards you.

Remember, the opponents will do everything they can to clear the ball away while it's in transit, so you have to be fast acting.

The higher the competition you face, the more important this becomes.

When I first started playing, I used to stand and wait for the ball to arrive, much like any other amateur player.

Once it was at my feet, I would then put it under control and make my approach towards the goal.

This worked just fine against my fellow rookie players, but as soon as I started to face professional defenders, my whole approach had to change, and change fast.

I can recall my first "serious" match.

I had barely received the ball, and there they all were, slide tackling me or clearing the ball away with ease, which was really frustrating.

It took a while before I realized that I needed to really up my game if I were to score any goals against players like these.

I started to be extra alert, more on my toes, and ready for faster, more aggressive soccer, not so much through choice, but through necessity.

So there I was again, only this time in movement as the ball was passed in my direction.

I noticed how moving towards the ball, as opposed to waiting for it to arrive at my feet, had improved my chance of scoring.

It also increased the time I had to finish the attack compared to previous passes, where the opponents caught up with me before I'd even got a chance to run with the ball.

Another thing I noticed about running with the ball was the benefit gained when opponents came late into a situation.

Now I could dodge them or cause them to make tackling mistakes far more easily, some of which could lead to penalties.

This is because they have less time to act and are therefore coerced into making faster, less controlled decisions.

For example, I would often perform a fake kick inside the penalty box as I was running with the ball.

The result of this could lead to a free kick, a one-on-one duel with the keeper, or the opponent attempting a slide tackle without the ball, which would get me a penalty kick.

To summarize this chapter: Receiving the ball while you are on the move has several advantages.

It is a really simple strategy that, once mastered, greatly increases your goal scoring opportunities.

Start using this approach in your very next game and get to discover how it gives you a real competitive edge over your opponents.

19 MOST ACCURATE PART OF THE FOOT

The inside part of the foot is not only the most powerful part to shoot with, but it is also the most accurate and effective for scoring goals.

A well-aimed shot using the inside part of the foot, and with sufficient power, will beat any keeper in the world when executed properly.

However, the worst thing you can do when shooting at the goal is to load your kick with all the power you can muster and just fire away, hoping the ball will burn the masks on its way to the back of the net.

These types of shots are for rookies, and smart goal scorers use less power, more accuracy, and most importantly, the inside part of their foot.

I always like to back up my explanations using professional soccer players to illustrate my points.

If you study any of the top scorers, you will notice that most of their goals are gained using the inside part of the foot.

They shoot like this for no other reason than it provides them with the most power, accuracy, and breadth needed for scoring great goals.

There was a time where I played with an incredibly good scorer, and this guy never used his instep to shoot.

I found his approach really interesting because he was scoring a lot of goals.

One day I asked him why he used the inside part of his foot all the time.

He just said that it's by far the most reliable and accurate part for scoring goals, and that's all he had to say on the subject.

He suggested I try using the inside of my foot so that I could see for myself how well this approach works.

I was not really persuaded by this so I continued with my power shots and decided to discard his advice!

Well, for someone who thought they knew best I sure as heck wasn't doing very well!

I mean, my high-powered kicks missed the goal more often than not, mostly because they were difficult to control because of the power I applied.

One day, more out of frustration than belief, I reluctantly decided to try the other approach.

After all, way things were going I had nothing to lose by at least having a go.

During one particular game I decided to only shoot using the inside part of my foot.

I also made a conscious decision not to use any more power than was necessary, no matter how tempting it might be.

My chance came in the second half where I got a rebound from a shot that one of my teammates fired.

I was just outside the 18 yard box when this happened.

Instead of striking the ball with full force (as I usually did), this time I deliberately aimed at the right post and gently released a more controlled shot.

I have to say it felt most unnatural, but the result totally surprised me.

As the keeper was three yards outside the goal line, the ball landed nicely in the top right corner.

Wow!

Suddenly, right there and then, I realized I had just scored! It seemed that "less" really did mean "more" and I had been proved wrong, very wrong!

From that day forward I decided to always use the inside foot and stop the power-shooting altogether whenever anywhere near the 18 yard box.

I made a vow with myself to only fire powerful shots when I was at least 25 yards from the penalty area.

As soon as I crossed that line, I would then switch to using the inside for all my scoring attempts.

If you don't already follow this rule, then I suggest you start right away.

This tactic will almost certainly work wonders for your scoring success, just as it has done for mine.

I am convinced that once you get to experience for yourself how effective this controlled way of shooting actually is, then you will stop firing unnecessarily powerful shots from within the penalty area.

20 SHOOT LOW AND SCORE

The reason why shooting low is so effective is because the keeper has to dive near the ground to save the ball, and this takes longer than when diving in the air.

If you can shoot low, and with sufficient power, then you will score more goals.

Most players focus far too much on curving the ball and shooting at full power.

Quite often though, a low kick using the inside part of the foot, is all that's required.

I agree that landing a well-aimed power-shot in the top right corner of the net looks great, but honestly, how often do attempts like these actually succeed?

Not very often, is the answer to that.

The reality is this: a low and accurate shot has a much higher potential of beating the keeper than a high strike.

There is also a much greater chance of a low ball reaching the goal. This is because it's a lot harder for the opponents to intercept.

You need to ask yourself whether it's more important for you to score goals that look impressive, or if it's more important to just score no matter what.

I used to play to impress, and so focused on scoring spectacular goals as often as I possibly could.

Time and again I would aim high and attempt to hit either the top right or top left corners.

Regrettably, these attempts to impress failed more often than they succeeded.

Obviously there were some successful goals – sometimes – but in reality I could have scored many more if only I had aimed low.

If you observe low shooting, you will see that plenty of shots from around 25 yards find their way past the keeper.

The reason for this is because a low ball travels very fast, and on a wet ground it accelerates with every yard.

Add to this the bounce aspect as the ball moves nearer the goal, and the chances of scoring become even greater.

As you can see, there are a number of factors with low shots that help to increase the chances of scoring.

There is certainly a higher potential for success compared to kicking hard and aiming high at one of the top corners.

It will be wise for you to pay close attention to low shooting.

Honestly, it can mean the difference between scoring lots of goals, very few or none at all.

My technique for scoring more goals using low shots is to always have the supporting foot point towards the target.

When you do this, the ball travels in the direction that the supporting foot is pointing.

It's also important to place the supporting foot in line with the ball and to bend forwards slightly in order to keep it low.

Additionally, use the inside-foot when inside the penalty area, and the instep (arched middle part of the foot between toes and ankle) if you are outside the penalty box.

Follow these tips and you are guaranteed to score more goals.

21 STUDY THE BEST EVER GOAL SCORERS

Every time I study great goalies as a way to help improve my own skills, it always amazes me just how much there is still to learn.

By the way, it's important to note that there's a huge difference between watching videos for entertainment and actually analyzing them for educational purposes.

Like every other soccer enthusiast, I also love to watch beautiful goals and be entertained with ball tricks.

Even so, I still diligently devote some time for analyzing my favorite players.

This way I get to constantly find out new things that I can then try to apply, and perhaps adapt, into my own game.

When I'm in "serious mode" I have a notepad by my side and write down anything I spot that professional players do well.

I also jot down those things that they may have flunked on.

By studying in this way, I am able to visualize how it might be possible to use something, or avoid something, as a method of improving my own goal scoring abilities.

While observing great goal scorers, I usually look for the smaller details that most players tend to overlook.

This might include such things as what he did before receiving the ball, how he received the ball, and how he followed through when finishing, etc.

My favorite player of all time is the now retired Brazilian super striker, often referred as the Il Fenomeno (Phenomenon), Ronaldo Luís Nazário de Lima.

In my opinion, he was, and remains to this day, to be the best goal scorer soccer has ever known. I have often studied him and looked closely at what he did in different situations.

As I examined him, I was not trying to imitate his skills per se.

I was simply attempting to single out why he did what he did in different goal scoring situations.

Things like, for example, what moves he performed when facing the keeper in one-on-one duels, or what maneuvers he would make when there was an opponent standing between him and the goal?

I picked up on how Ronaldo would often finish on one-touch, and I also noticed that he would often shoot low to the ground.

Something else that caught my attention was how he frequently performed a small body feint just before finishing an attack.

This seemed to work really well at confusing nearby opponents, and the keeper.

When you study the tactical moves of a great goal scorer, be sure to pick someone you believe is an inspiration to you personally.

Scrutinize him closely, and write down whatever you think he's doing right.

Also make notes of anything you spot that you think was a bad move or poor choice at the time.

Writing notes is a very effective way to reinforce the learning process, so be sure to have paper and pencil handy before you view any footage.

Once you have logged your observations, try to use what you have discovered to help develop your own goal scoring skills.

In order to carry out this exercise with any real success you must be able to constructively criticize your own method of play.

Never be too proud to admit your shortcomings as and when you pick up on them.

If you are not scoring goals, or not scoring as often as you think you should be, then there will be areas of your game that need improving.

Studying talented goal scorers is a very good way to indirectly find flaws within your own game.

22 BEHIND AND IN FRONT OF DEFENDERS IN THE BOX

Being in front of the defender, as opposed to being behind him as the ball is played inside the 18 yard box, is another of those deciding factors that can influence whether a goal scoring opportunity will succeed or fail.

This is especially important for low-crossed balls, and if you fail to get in front of the opponents, then your chances of scoring will be greatly reduced.

However, there is an exception to this rule when it comes to headers.

When there is the potential for a header shot, it can be more beneficial to stand about half a yard behind your opponent.

If he fails to head the ball, then you get an ideal chance to head it yourself straight into the goal.

I need to raise a word of caution here though. I am not saying that you should simply stand in front or behind an opponent.

There is no hard or fixed rule with this.

What you need to do is to keep moving all the time, and as the ball is being played, you should intuitively pick the best position based on whether it's crossed high or low.

Here is how I play when a ball is crossed low.

Every time my winger prepares to cross the ball inside the box, I move back and forth, left to right, and basically do everything I can to confuse the opponent marking me.

As the ball is crossed, I wait until it's about half way towards me and then jump quickly in front of the opponent.

I also use my elbows to shield my respective sides and to prevent the opponent from getting a touch on the ball.

Warning!

Try not to raise your elbows too high. If you do, then you run the risk of getting yourself a red card because there's a potential danger of hitting your opponents head.

If you keep them below shoulder level you will be just fine.

When it comes to high-crossed balls, I position myself as close as possible to the opponent.

Once the ball is about half way through the air, I then move backwards about half a yard to allow myself enough space to perform a jump header.

Quite often, an opponent will miss to chance to clear the ball with a header because there will be several other players involved in the duel.

I have scored a good few goals using my approach, despite being a fairly short player, so I know this works.

To summarize this chapter:

Make sure you don't just read what I've written here and then forget about it later.

Realize that my tips and suggestions will only work if you work at them.

Follow my advice and it's inevitable that your goal scoring will improve.

23 BEING AT THE RIGHT PLACE AT RIGHT TIME

You must have heard about the importance of being in the right spot at the right time, especially when it comes to scoring spectacular goals.

Some folks claim that being a great goal scorer is a rare talent, and something that you are either born with or you're not, but I disagree.

Okay, so some players are naturally talented, but I firmly believe that those who are not can still develop their skills to great effect, so long as they are passionate and dedicated.

One way of keeping motivated and focused, is to always believe that the ball will find its way through the players and land at your feet, but for this to happen you have keep moving with the game.

I know from experience that the correct attitude and flow will always find you in the right spot at the right time, and that means a plenty of opportunities to score.

The secret for getting yourself in the right place at the right time is actually no secret at all!

You simply need to calculate the probability of where the ball is likely to be at any given time.

Something well worth remembering is that one of the most common goal scoring situations is when the ball is crossed from the side.

It's important that you get into the habit of thinking on your toes.

When you learn how to instinctively figure out whether a ball will be cleared, rebounded, or find its way through the defenders towards your direction, then you have surely developed one of soccer's major skills.

The higher the competition you face in soccer, the fewer chances you get to score.

Therefore, the more skills you can get under your belt, the better your odds become.

There was a time where I would wait about two to three yards from the penalty box line, just hoping against hope for a rebound as the ball was crossed inside the box.

The reasons why I stood here was because I once scored indirectly from that position, and because of that I believed it was the best place to put myself whenever the ball was crossed inside.

As it turned out, this was not the pole position I thought it was.

The few times the ball did find its way over to me, it was usually bouncing erratically, and that made it difficult to get control of and perform an accurate kick.

Striking the ball without any real control often saw my scoring attempts end up some 30 yards or so behind the goal.

It wasn't until I came across a documentary about the world's best strikers, that I was able to pick up on why I failed to score so often.

These strikers all agreed that the secret for scoring plenty of goals was to be in the right place at the right time.

It suddenly dawned on me that I must be in the wrong place, most of the time.

These players also said that it's important to be as close to the ball as possible, and to also be confident that the ball can, and probably will, find its way through the defenders and over to you at some point.

For this to happen though, you must keep yourself close to the action.

If you don't believe in this, and stay on the fringes, then you will rarely score any goals, not least because you're unprepared, and probably too far away from the ball.

I listened to their advice intently and took what they said literally.

From the very next game I began to stay as close to the ball as possible; believing it would find its way through all the opponents towards me, providing I stayed with it.

I started to score really simple goals by just touching the ball, and the more I scored, the more I believed anything was possible, and so it was!

24 TIMING YOUR SCORING ATTEMPTS

The better you can time your goal scoring attempts the easier it will be for you to finish an attack with a single kick.

In professional soccer there just isn't time to jog around and set up the ball as you would like to.

Timing is really important because it can make or break goal scoring attempts.

The key is to know what speed to approach the ball, and that means being careful not to go in too fast or too slow.

Perfecting timing might sound complicated, but it's actually just another skill to learn, and once grasped, you will be able to execute it without too much conscious thought.

Perhaps the easiest way to comprehend the importance of timing is for you to visualize yourself performing a jump header.

In this situation, jumping too early or too late will result in a failure, unless the ball finds its way into the goal by way of a fluke; something that obviously can't be relied on!

On the other hand, if you jump at exactly the right moment then you will get a good clean header, and one that is easier to control.

Heading the ball at just the right moment obviously has a much better chance of finding its way into the goal too.

The header scenario is a good way to illustrate the importance of timing, so let's now look at how to go about improving this skill.

Perfecting your timing is no different to developing any other skill, in that you have to practice and apply to get good at it.

The more you do this the better you become; it really is as simple as that.

Having good timing is something that truly separates professionals from amateurs.

Once I began to play against professional players, I quickly realized that I would need to improve my timing if I wanted to score any goals at all.

The very first goal I scored against professional opponents was with a jumping header.

After that, I spent a week practicing on nothing else but timing the crosses.

Getting the timing right is essential to all scoring situations and attempts.

Whether you are shooting on a rebound, jumping for a header, or the ball is bouncing towards you uncontrollably, timing your moves is fundamental to the outcome.

While you practice, make sure to maintain good focus as you approach the ball.

Try to shut out any other thoughts or distractions as you work at hardwiring good timing into you conscious mind.

Don't concentrate so hard though that you get into microanalysis mode because that will only hinder your progress.

Just know what you have to do and go at it until such times that you intuitively know how to time your goal scoring opportunities.

To summarize this chapter: Practice makes perfect. Set yourself some challenges and keep working at them.

As your timing improves it will gradually become more natural and less conscious.

The more you are able to time your goal scoring opportunities precisely, the more goals you will end up scoring.

25 INVOLVE YOUR MATES

When you watch professional soccer games, notice how top strikers always involve their teammates as they approach the goal.

A typical sequence is where the defenders play the ball up to the striker who then plays it back to the midfielder as he takes up a new position.

They play like this as it's so much easier to work as a team in these situations, not least because it allows the striker to gain extra yards as he approaches the opponent's goal.

In other words, it's a faster method than trying to play solo.

The higher the competition, the more important this kind of tactical play becomes.

I often liked to do things solo, in much the same way as I would during practice sessions or a friendly kick-around with mates.

In these situations I could quite easily dribble past five opponents and still manage to score.

Nonetheless, such playfulness has no place in real competition.

It was only when I became a better player, and the competition got a lot more competitive, that I realized the true importance of cooperation on the field.

I certainly had to change my ways and start using the team to better advantage when competing in serious games.

In my ignorance, I initially thought that having less control of the ball would see a drop in goal-scoring opportunities, but much to my surprise the opposite was true.

I saw that the more I involved my teammates in an advance towards the goal, the easier and faster it was for me to race ahead and prepare myself.

This style of play put me in a far more favorable position where I got to score more goals more often.

My special strategy was to receive the ball, pass it to one of the wingers, and then race ahead and take up a new position in the penalty box.

The reason this worked so well was because I was able to get the first touch on the ball, but not only that.

This approach also succeeded because the wingers were really good at serving me with some great passes from which I could score from.

Without these team efforts I would not have scored half of the goals that I did.

In soccer, it's vital that you embrace the concept of teamwork. When a team plays well as a single unit they become so much harder to beat.

Take Germany with their 2014 FIFA World Cup squad.

They might not have had the best players on the planet, but they certainly had the best team, and that's why they won.

When Germany competed, the team was in sync and their game ran like a well-oiled machine.

If you're a rookie who has only just started to play soccer, then embrace the team concept from the outset and make sure you involve other players in the game.

If you are more experienced, yet can identify yourself as someone who plays a solo game, then this is one habit you just have to break.

It doesn't really matter how good you are, or think you might be, you must avoid hogging the ball and going solo, and if you don't, then your attempts will result in far more failures than successes.

As I mentioned before, playing solo all the time might work against opponents that are really poor, or when you're having a bit of a kick-around with friends, but as soon as you start to face more serious challengers in aggressive competitions, then you will surely wish you hadn't developed the habit of hogging the ball.

My coach would often emphasize the true importance of teamwork.

He would point out how we could play better, faster, and be presented with more scoring opportunities, simply by sharing the ball.

He was right, of course!

Anyone who is serious about becoming a successful soccer player has to understand that less time with the ball brings about more goal scoring opportunities.

26 DARE TO TAKE ON DEFENDERS

Taking on defenders in a one-on-one situation, and successfully getting past them, is no easy feat.

However, it is a very important skill to master if you want to become a true goal-scoring machine.

A player who can get past his opponents and finish the shot is a real nightmare for any defender.

Such advice is all too often misunderstood and often gets interpreted as a suggestion to dribble as soon as you have a goal scoring opportunity.

Instead, this approach should be looked at as one where you choose your options carefully.

Like all soccer moves, whether or not you should take on defenders in a duel is something that calls for quick and decisive decision making.

When I first started to play serious soccer I rarely thought about dribbling my opponents. Whenever I could, I'd usually pass the ball on as soon as I received it.

Even when I was completely alone and confronted by only one opponent between me and the goal, I would still attempt to pass the ball over to a teammate, even if he was marked by several rival players.

This irrational behavior caused me to lose out on a lot of scoring opportunities. My teammates were often irritated whenever I passed the ball instead of challenging opponents.

My reason for doing this is not an unfamiliar one among lesser-experienced players, as I was at the time.

I simply did not have the courage to invite opponents to a one-on-one duel, especially when playing against an aggressive and experienced team.

Today is another story. I always look for a way to challenge any opponent in a one-one-one duel, especially when they are the only obstacle between me and the goal.

Nowadays I relish these situations. In fact, challenging opponents in one-on-one duels, and hopefully following through to the finish, is one of the things I love to do most on the soccer field.

A lot of players don't realize that when they have the ball and are confronted in a one-to-one situation, it is they who are in pole position.

This is especially true when there is only one opponent remaining between them and the goal.

In many situations, performing a single body feint will be enough to shake off the defender.

Even so, none of this advice is of any use unless you dare to follow through with it.

I know it took me a while to pluck up the courage, but it all turned out to be so much easier and far more enjoyable, than I ever could have imagined!

I have played as a defender in my time, and I know from firsthand experience how daunting it can be when faced with a fast approaching player who is known to be good at dribbling.

In situations like these there is only one chance to clear that ball.

A failed attempt basically gives the opponent a free run at the goal.

Charging towards the goal with the ball puts you at a huge advantage over a defending opponent.

He wants what you have, or at least he wants to clear it from your feet, and that is why you must dare to challenge him.

Of course you will fail sometimes, but with the right physical and mental approach, you will succeed far more often and score many more goals.

To summarize this chapter: If you're fearful about taking on defenders in one-on-one duels then find a way to overcome this immediately.

Ask for help and guidance if you need to, but don't put this off.

Honestly, you will find that any fears you might have will all turn out to be a lot of fuss over nothing.

The more you dare, the more you will want to challenge.

Overcoming this setback will not only make you a better player, but you will also get to enjoy your games a whole lot more as well.

27 AIM FOR THE CLOSEST POST

One of the best tactics I've learned for scoring goals from balls crossed into the penalty box, is to try and get as near the post that is closest to the ball.

For example, if the cross is from the right, then I would move towards the right post as it's the closest to the ball.

The way to successfully execute this strategy is to wait until the ball has crossed inside the penalty box, and then quickly run in the direction of the post.

The better your timing, the higher your chances of scoring become.

Also worth noting is that the more you can disguise your intentions, the less you will have to grapple with defenders as you race into position.

The worst thing you can do is get into position too early. The consequence of this is that you will probably miss the ball or get caught between two opponents.

A handy little trick I use to successfully avoid this scenario is to run in a zigzag fashion.

Running like this is great as an avoidance maneuver.

All you have to do is to first run off in one direction to get the opponents following.

Then as the ball is crossed over, you quickly change course and head towards its direction.

This move works really well at shaking off any opponents that were on your tail.

It does takes a bit of practice, but once you become adept at it, I can assure you that this is going to be something that will prove to be very effective.

To illustrate this further, let's say one of my teammates is preparing to cross the ball inside the penalty area.

What I would do is to run a few yards from the 18 yard box towards the opponent's goal.

This run should be in the general direction of the opposite post.

That means if the ball is crossed from the right, I would first head for the left post.

This run would be performed at about half of my maximum speed.

Then as the ball is crossed over, I quickly change direction and run towards the right post.

If I had timed my run well, then I would meet the ball at just the right moment, thus enabling me to strike it perfectly using the inside part of my foot.

Providing everything goes according to plan, the ball should find its way past the keeper and I get to add yet another goal to my goal-scoring statistic.

As you can see, this is not a fancy skill or some highly advanced ball handling technique, but merely a simple, yet highly effective, calculated maneuver.

The power generated from the cross is usually enough to beat the keeper as long as you meet it at the right time.

By using this strategy, I have been able to score many goals throughout my career, especially against opponents that were not clever enough to understand what my intentions were at the time.

If I were you, I would start implementing this strategy into my tactical arsenal right away.

It really is a simple yet effective way to increase your goal scoring opportunities.

If, after you've practiced and tried this a number of times, and still don't manage to score from it, then you are either timing the ball poorly, running to slow, or not disguising your intentions well enough from the surrounding opponents.

In order to find out the root cause of your failures, you will have to do a little self-analysis and make adjustments wherever necessary.

28 SHOOT DURING A RUN

If you are anything like I was, there will be nothing you like better than to receive the ball and set it up nicely before releasing a well-aimed missile at the opponent's goal.

It feels great when the luxury of time is on your side, but as I've pointed out previously, this is not a realistic approach in competitive soccer.

When you are facing a skillful team, time is always of the essence.

There will rarely be a moment where you don't have at least one opponent on your back.

He may try to slide-tackle, push you off balance, or use some other sneaky trick to mess with your game.

When I started to play senior football at the age of 16, I noticed right away that the game I had been used to was about to change forever.

Suddenly, my opponents were stronger, faster, and incredibly good at tackling when compared to those in junior leagues.

At the start, I continued with my old shooting pattern, not least because it was all I knew.

I would receive the ball and attempt to set it up nicely in preparation for a well-aimed shot.

As much as I had always enjoyed playing this way, it didn't take me long to realize that it was now one of a number of approaches that I had to be rid of, and quickly!

This was not a habit that took too long to break either because the second I got the ball, the opponents would clear it away – every single time!

My solution to this problem was to shoot while on the move.

This new approach, once mastered, allowed me to release a well-aimed shot even when I had an opponent or two hot on my heels.

I discovered that it was also much harder for opponents to clear the ball away when I'm moving.

So on the whole, my game began to adapt and mature quite nicely to senior soccer.

The one disadvantage with this scoring strategy is that you will often release unintentionally powerful shots with your instep.

Using the instep makes it much harder to control the ball. Therefore, it's always a good idea to try and keep the ball low and aim at one of the posts.

I found this approach to be a great way to play successful soccer, especially in fast-paced games where there is serious competition.

This technique is even good for 30-yard shots. This is especially so when the ground is wet because the ball gains more speed as it bounces along the surface.

Make sure you vary your shots sometimes too by aiming high.

The reason you should diverge occasionally is because striking the ball in exactly the same way – constantly – runs the risk of turning you into a predictable player, and you don't want that!

In case you're not familiar with how to keep the ball low, all you need to do is lean slightly forward as you release the shot.

If you want to have the ball go higher, then the opposite is true, and you simply lean slightly backwards before striking the ball.

You will need to practice a bit on this because there's a risk of overdoing things until you get comfortable with controlled shooting.

One thing I also do is reduce my speed a bit before releasing the shot.

This helps me to get the ball where I want it to go.

Obviously there's no time for slowing down when there's an opponent on your back though, as that would give him an opportunity to clear the ball.

To summarize this chapter: This is a strategy that can be used irrespective of which position you play. It is yet another skill that, once mastered, will contribute to your goal scoring statistics.

It shouldn't take you too long to become proficient at this either, but you will want to practice a bit before trying it out in actual competition.

29 TAKE ADVANTAGE OF THE WET FIELD

As I look back on my soccer career, I notice that most of my goals were scored during wet weather.

That might sound odd, especially when you consider how hard it can be to score when a soccer field is drenched in water.

Even so, my scoring success was no coincidence. In this chapter I will give you three great tips on how to utilize a wet soccer pitch.

The first tip is to shoot as much as possible, and I really do mean that you should shoot more often than you normally would.

When ground conditions are sodden, even a poor shot can result in a goal.

I've seen really mediocre attempts to score beat very skillful keepers, and all because the ground was wet and muddy.

You should pick your shooting opportunities wisely though.

Don't just aim at the goal for the sake of it because even wet conditions require some degree of control and skill.

All the same, feel free to be less careful than you would where the conditions are more favorable.

Don't be afraid to take a shot from 30 yards or further, just to test the keeper's ability to save in wet conditions.

Although the chances of scoring from long distances are low, remember that the ball is going to be incredibly hard to grip; something that is in your favor and a disadvantage to the keeper.

Not being able to get a good hold on the ball is what sees a lot of goals through; goals that would never have made it under normal conditions.

My second tip is to keep the shot as low as possible.

The reason for this is because the ball gains more speed on wet ground.

So the faster the ball moves towards the goal, the harder it is to save.

Quite often the goalie is taken by surprise at the speed of the approaching ball and subsequently miscalculates his dive.

The key point to consider here is to shoot at the corner furthest away from where the keeper is standing whenever you can.

Keep in mind the fact that the goalie needs twice as much time to dive for a low ball as he does one aimed at chest level.

In short, a well-executed low-shot directed at the corner furthest from the keeper vastly improves your chances of scoring, particularly in wet conditions.

The third tip for scoring on a wet pitch is to have your shots bounce at least once before they reach the goal.

The best way to achieve this is to strike the ball with a lot of power, and keep it as low to the ground as possible.

If you can achieve this, then the ball should bounce a few times as it travels towards the goal.

Just remember, a fast bouncing ball on a wet surface has a good probability of beating the keeper so long as the aim is accurate.

Bouncing shots are a real nightmare for goalies because the path of the ball is impossible to predict.

This is why you regularly see professional keepers looking beaten and befuddled by shots that appear so amateur that even a raw beginner should have been able to block them.

Although these goals look unbelievably ridiculous, embarrassing for the goalkeeper even, you would have to actually be in goal yourself to fully understand why they can be so difficult to save.

If you want some prime examples of this phenomenon, then try searching for "goalkeeper bloopers" on YouTube.

One thing you will notice is how many of these apparent gaffes occurred during bad weather.

Besides giving you a good laugh, these examples will hopefully convince you to start using my "Playing on a Wet Field" tips to your own advantage.

To summarize this chapter: These three tips are what helped me score at least one goal per game when the field was wet.

If it's actually raining as well, you will have even more success providing you keep your wits about you.

Most players don't relish the thought of competing in miserable weather, but can, now that you know how to turn this to your advantage.

Just keep in mind that wet fields add another level of difficulty for goalkeepers attempting to block the ball.

Retain this detail and you too will soon be chalking up your goals statistic when playing in poor conditions.

30 INSIDE OF POSTS

As you probably already know, curving the ball in order to get it near the post is a really effective skill to have.

There is, however, something else that's really effective, and it's my guess you don't know about it...yet!

In this chapter I will be revealing this little known secret to you. Before I continue though, I will just mention that this is something that took my aiming accuracy from <u>average</u> to <u>exceptional</u>.

I always tried hard at curving the ball, and getting it to arc was never a problem, but for some reason these attempts mostly landed in the middle of the goal.

The curves were usually perfect, but hitting the target area was the problem.

One day as I was practicing, one of the former big players of our club was watching us train when suddenly he called me to the side.

When I jogged over he asked whether I wanted to know how to successfully curve the ball and get it right on target?

Before I got a chance to reply he was gone.

He'd ran onto the training pitch and placed the ball about 25 yards from the goal.

He then took a bet with our keeper that he would score; despite the fact he was wearing jogging shoes.

Without further ado, he fired the shot and the ball curved perfectly at the just right moment.

The goal was his!

This was an impressive goal to say the least, although the keeper didn't look too awestruck!

He then turned back to me and explained that the way to curve the ball and have it enter the goal near the posts is to look and aim half a yard past the post you're targeting.

So this meant if I were shooting at the right post I would aim a half yard away to the right of it (as if I were purposely trying to miss the target).

I had a hard time grasping this concept, so the only way to know if he was pulling my leg or not was to test it.

Well, the very first shot was amazing and I couldn't believe how successful this strategy was.

Even though I clipped the post on that first attempt, I was still overjoyed because the theory was proven.

All I had to do now was perfect the curve slightly so that it coincided with the aim and edged just inside the post, as opposed to bouncing off it.

This new approach had me hitting the posts nine times out of ten from the outset, and that to me, was truly amazing.

So with a little tweaking, my goal scoring endeavors were guaranteed to move up to a whole new level, all thanks to a better player passing on his experience.

When people see how well I can shoot today I can tell that they are genuinely impressed.

It's not uncommon for folks to approach me and ask how I manage to hit the ball just inside the posts on almost every attempt.

Somewhat selfishly, I just laugh and say that I've spent a lot of time practicing.

Even though I do practice a lot, I never reveal the little secret that allows me to score with such impressive accuracy.

Seeing as you've purchased my book though, I am more than happy to share this with you.

Just make sure you try it out for yourself, and don't worry if you don't hack it right away.

I can guarantee that with a little practice, you too will take your goal scoring up to a whole new level.

31 DIVE, SCORE AND AVOID INJURIES

The first time I ever scored a goal with a diving header, I wondered afterwards if this had been a brave or really stupid action due to the risk of getting accidentally kicked in the head.

I learned later that it's not as risky as first thought when done correctly.

That doesn't mean this way of scoring goals carries no dangers, because it does, obviously, but I will explain in this chapter how you can vastly reduce the risk of injury.

Sometimes, a diving header is the only option available if you want to score a goal.

Situations that call for a diving header are when the ball is too far from your legs to get a good strike, and travelling too low for a standard header.

Typically, these situations occur when the ball is crossed from the wings, but they can also appear suddenly if the opponents fail to clear the ball away.

The reason I have been able to score numerous goals using this technique, and without injury, is because I have always quickly evaluated the situation before acting.

Whenever I think there's a risk of an opponent's boot striking my head, I simply avoided any temptation to dive.

Another thing I do is to always keep my arms outstretched in order to add some additional protection.

This is especially useful if there's an opponent nearby who decides to try and clear the ball away with his foot.

If this does happen, then it's better to get kicked in the arms rather than the head.

Something else worth pointing out is to never close your eyes during impact with the ball.

If you do, then you won't be able to see what's going on in front of you, and that's asking for trouble!

If there's an opponent's being thrust towards you, then you will want to know about it so that you can shield yourself. Obviously you can't act if you're heading the ball with closed eyes.

Once you decide to perform a diving header, then it has to be done with real determination and as much power as you can muster.

Anything less is destined to fail. Make sure you are mindful of your aim as well, and not just head the ball for the sake of it.

I will now outline a strategy that has worked very well for me during my soccer career.

As the ball is about to be crossed inside the penalty box, I start by taking a step backwards so as to get the opponent(s) move along with me.

Then, as the ball is crossed inside the penalty box, I move towards the goal and time the header so that I'm already in the air as the ball approaches me.

So long as I time everything right, I can then make a good clean contact with my forehead.

Note that the power from the cross will be more than enough to head the ball with sufficient force.

And by keeping my eyes open I am able to take aim and hopefully beat the keeper.

32 IN FRONT OF THE SHOT

This is probably the easiest way of scoring a goal with the minimum of effort.

The only requirement is that you put yourself in front of the shooter and hope the ball bounces off you.

The aim is not to steal the goal, as such, but to have the ball redirect off of you thus causing the keeper to dive in the wrong direction.

You will have most success with this strategy during direct free kicks or when there is a rebound from a corner kick.

In these situations you are generally closer to the ball, and this increases the chance of it being redirected as it hits you.

There is one player I would like you to look at to help better illustrate this scoring strategy.

He is the former A.C Milan striker, Filippo Inzaghi. This guy was incredible at this.

He would often put himself in front of a shot in an attempt to have the ball redirect off him.

He would frequently score doing this too!

Check the first goal of the Champions League Final in 2007 against Liverpool.

Here you will see where Inzaghi got the ball to redirect off him from a direct kick performed by Andrea Pirlo.

He ran into the path of the ball, got hit on the back, and then just watched as it rolled over the goal line. What a classic!

This is just one of many examples of how well this strategy can work.

Putting yourself in the right place at the right time will surely improve your goal scoring stats significantly when done properly.

The funny thing is that even if you try hiding yourself, you could still score like this proving you quickly move into the right spot just when it matters.

During a game once, I remember lying on the ground as one of my teammates was about to release a shot from a corner rebound.

Despite me trying to avoid the ball in this particular instance, it struck me hard on the side of the head, thus changing its course.

Much to all of our surprise, that ball landed neatly in the back of the net.

However, it's important to understand that there is also a risk of preventing an ideal goal scoring opportunity if you get hit by the ball while standing in the wrong place at the wrong time.

I have experienced this a few times in my career and it's really frustrating.

Sometimes a block may even look as though you are trying to prevent your teammate from scoring a goal, even though you're not.

Because soccer can be such a fast paced game, there will be times where moving out of the way can actually put you in the way, resulting in the ball hitting you and veering of course.

You will likely face a lot of uncertainty with this scoring strategy as you never quite know whether a shot will hit you in the leg, torso or head, let alone which direction the ball might take.

But when you think a situation warrants it then you must go with your gut.

I have scored some good goals in my time doing this, and consequently helped lead my team to victory because of those decisions.

33 AVOIDING OFFSIDE TRAPS

The only way to score goals against strong competition is to learn how to successfully avoid offside traps.

I will assume you already know what offside is, so I will not get into discussing the rules of that here.

Instead, I will move straight on to the strategy I use to beat a strong defense.

This maneuver is actually quite basic in its approach.

What I do is to move myself back by one yard just before the ball is passed over.

This means I have the last standing player one yard in front of me.

This extra yard gives me an opportunity to gain some extra speed as the ball is crossed, and also prevents me getting into the offside trap.

Standing in line with the last opponent will usually get you offside as he will move up in the field and leave you behind him just before the ball is passed.

There is nothing more frustrating than having an open road towards the goal just to hear the referee blow his whistle as the line ref indicates offside with his flag.

I've already discussed Filippo Inzaghi in this book, but I can't avoid doing it again here to help illustrate my point.

He was a real master at avoiding offside, but he was also one of the players who commentators jested must have been born in offside.

I mean, he would run into offside so many times that referees got tired of blowing their whistles, and side refs got pains in their arms by raising their flags so often.

Yet despite it all, this player scored so many goals that you would need several days to watch them all, which illustrates the true importance of being able to avoid offside traps.

I know it is easy give in to temptation and begin your run before the ball is passed – as you are in line with the opponent – but you need to be smart and keep yourself calm in these situations.

Remember also that the opponent will usually need to turn around and start his run after you; something that gives you a big advantage over him.

I have never been what you might call a fast player, yet I managed to score many goals by utilizing this strategy.

In other words, you will have even more success if you are a fast-paced player, but even if you are below average, don't worry!

You will still get to score more goals by following the tips outlined in this chapter.

34 THE POWER OF YOUR HEEL

Using the heel to score goals is most likely something you haven't thought about, but it can be really effective if you use it in the right circumstances.

One of these situations is when you find yourself facing the wrong way inside the penalty area with several opponents behind you making it impossible to turn around and get a clean shot.

In these situations the power of heel cannot be emphasized enough.

Here, you have a great opportunity to release a surprise kick, and with enough power to beat the keeper.

The key to scoring this way is to disguise your intention from those around you. It's also important to create enough space around you to strike the ball with plenty of power.

I generally receive the ball with the sole of my foot while shielding the area with my arms.

Once I have the ball under control, I then raise my leg as high as possible and then release it quickly.

This is the best way to generate the power necessary for a good kick.

It's also more effective to strike the ball in the middle if you can, as this helps to keep it in a straight line as it travels toward the goal.

The great thing with this scoring strategy is the element of surprise, not least with the keeper.

The goalie will often react too late simply because he wasn't expecting to see the ball. I've scored several goals this way and it's incredibly satisfying.

You will have even more success if you are able to turn your head quickly just before taking the shot as this lets you check the position of the keeper ahead of the strike.

I would say that the preferable distance for heel shots is not more than 15 yards from the opponent's goal.

Any further than 15 yards and it becomes more difficult to generate a kick powerful enough to score with.

Long distance heel shots might work against weak competition, but they stand little chance of succeeding against serious competition.

Not every opportunity for a heel shot should be taken though just because it's possible.

In many cases, the safest option will be to pass the ball on to a better placed teammate who is facing in the right direction.

There's a good chance that he will be able to finish with an instep or inside shot, both of which are more likely to succeed than the heel.

However, in order to score more goals you must be prepared to take risks as and when situations demand it.

Therefore, I suggest you only execute the heel strategy when there are no unmarked teammates available to pass the ball to, and when nearby opponents prevent you from turning around to make a clear shot at the goal.

35 KEEPER MISTAKES

Most players bow their head after a missed goal and then turn away as they jog home in preparation for the opponent's keeper to reinstate the game.

A smart player will do things a little differently, however.

He will begin to retreat, but still have an unobvious eye firmly fixed on the goalie as he prepares his next move.

Most goalkeepers make mistakes sooner or later, especially when they bounce the ball on the ground as they figure out what to do next.

Sometimes a bouncing ball will hit a rut and rebound back into play.

Other times, a keeper will lose his grip on the ball, and once again it finds its way back into play.

These are just two examples of how a keeper can stumble.

The strategy therefore, is to always keep an eye on the goalie right up until the ball is reinstated back into play.

I have actually scored a few easy goals when keepers have slipped on the ground as they went to clear the ball.

Another situation I've scored from on occasion has been when a keeper misthrows the ball and it lands – unintentionally – right at my feet.

Slipups like these may happen quite often or quite rarely, depending on a number of things such as weather conditions, the level of competition, how focused the keeper is on the day, and so on.

I've played in games where keepers have made countless mistakes and others where they made none at all.

The point is to always expect the unexpected.

Constantly be vigilant and prepared for unanticipated events, and recognize the fact that they can, and often do, occur.

Be mindful of this and you will get to score more goals.

To summarize this chapter: Always, and I really do mean "always" have one eye on the keeper, even if he seems to have a firm grip on the ball and both feet securely attached to his torso.

He is only human, and that means he could lose focus and drop that ball at any time.

And if you're prepared for the unexpected, you may well get to score from a goalkeeper's slip and help your team to victory!

36 OPENING UP FOR SCORING

The game without the ball is equally important as the game with it.

In order to score goals you will need to be able to create scoring opportunities even when you don't have the ball at your feet.

I know from experience that I would not have scored half as many goals if I hadn't opened up scoring opportunities during the games.

A player who constantly strives to open up scoring opportunities is much harder to play against than someone who never does this.

He also scores more goals because he gets to receive additional passes from his teammates.

When I first started out playing soccer, this is something that used to confuse me.

I would often hear teammates shouting and beckoning me to open up for them, but I just couldn't grasp what they meant.

It wasn't until about a year later that I got to really understand what they wanted me to do, and once I did, my goal scoring potential escalated.

It is vital to realize just how important playing the game without the ball is for creating scoring opportunities.

Also be aware that a soccer player usually has the ball at his feet for two minutes on average, which means he will be playing for 88 minutes without it.

So that means there are 88 minutes of any given game where there is other work to do, and that time should be used to open up scoring breaks.

If you don't, then you will join the ranks of those players that rarely score any goals.

One of the best examples of a professional player, who made opening up scoring opportunities a fine art, is the former Bayern Munich striker, Jürgen Klinsmann.

He was never great at dribbling, nor was his shooting skill exceptional, but this was a player who was simply amazing when it came to opening up scoring chances.

Klinsmann scored a countless number of goals during his career by running into free space, which frequently gave his teammates an alternative area to pass the ball.

Although he often got himself caught offside, he also scored a lot of goals which made it all worthwhile.

The way Klinsmann played is clear proof that you don't have to possess exceptional shooting, dribbling or passing skills to become a good all-round tactical player.

Just as important is the ability to read the game well and open up scoring breaks as often as possible.

37 RECORDING YOUR PERFORMANCE

The first time I watched a videotape of myself was a game where I managed to score three goals.

I spent the whole day pushing the rewind button!

Not only was it nice to watch myself doing so well, but I actually couldn't believe it was me scoring these goals.

It was amazing to observe one of my shots which landed a goal from 30 yards.

This really boosted my desire to become an even better player and strive to score many more goals in future.

One of my friends, who enjoyed watching soccer more than playing it, used to come and support my teams in most of our games.

So one day I simply asked him if he would record my performance, but only during those times where I actually got control of the ball.

The reason for this was because I wanted to focus mainly on my ball skills and goal scoring.

Over time I got quite a collection of these tapes so I arranged them using a simple rating system.

Games where I didn't score a goal got one star, and games where I scored at least two goals would get a five star rating.

For each individual game, I would note down which parts of the body were used to score the goals.

I would log this data onto a simple spreadsheet where I had columns for **Feet**, **Head** and **Other**.

This helped me to quickly and easily identify where my strengths were and which areas needed improvement.

For example, by recording my performances and evaluating them afterwards, I soon got to notice that I rarely scored goals with my head, despite there being opportunities for header shots.

So, I decided to put more focus on improving my heading skills which eventually resulted in more goals for me.

The recording method is something I learned early on from a coach.

This guy really knew his stuff and once played for the Swedish national team.

He told me that a player can improve his scoring skills significantly by meticulously studying himself on video.

He said that reviewing my performance in this way would enable me to see "exactly" what I did during the game.

Moreover, he explained that this method is effective because it allows you to study when the mind is relaxed, recharged, and in learning mode.

He also said that it would give me new ideas on how to score more goals by tweaking existing skills that I get to examine in detail, thanks to the recordings.

I have never regretted taking his advice on recording my performance.

In fact, I doubt I would have developed to the level I did without employing this approach.

I understand that some players see this as too much microanalysis, or overkill, and I can see how they might think like that.

I would, however, urge everyone to at least try and record a couple of games.

After that, you can decide for yourself how useful you find it, and how far you want to go with this as a self-improvement tool.

If you are a keen amateur player, but don't hold any big dreams of building a professional soccer career, then you can happily skip this.

But if you are serious about your game, and your ambition is to become a goal scoring machine, then this is one strategy that you need to start paying close attention to.

38 TAKE HELP FROM TEAMMATES

I bet there is at least one player in your team, or a local team that you support, who is really good at scoring goals.

I bet too that you have often wondered how he manages to score time and again.

Well, those who wonder are the ones with tight lips, and those who know are those who dare to inquire.

There is nothing to be afraid of by asking for help and advice from players that are more experienced than you.

All it takes to start a conversation is a simple "Hi."

I once played alongside someone who was a real goal scoring prodigy and the envy of us all.

Honestly, this guy could produce the most amazing goals from nothing and nowhere.

One day, as we were meeting for a game, I asked him how I could improve my own goal scoring.

He pondered for a moment before saying that he had noticed I had a habit of overdoing things, and that I should try to simplify the way I played. I asked what he meant by "overdoing things?"

He explained that when I receive the ball I tend to take my time setting it up before deciding where best to aim.

This he thought, is what's hindering my progress.

He went on to say that there is simply no time for careful deliberation in real games, especially against strong competition, and that I have to learn how to act faster and keep with the flow.

He ended by saying that any reluctance to change would prevent me from developing my ability to score more goals.

Well, no player likes to hear strong criticism about the way they play, even when it is said in a constructive manner, but despite this, I knew he was right.

So, I had no choice but to take it all on the chin; something that turned out to be one of the best decisions I ever made.

My habit of setting the ball up before shooting proved to be a hard one to break, so I didn't start scoring more goals right away. But over the weeks and months that followed, the changes became evident as my goal scoring stats began to rise very nicely.

If you could use a little advice but don't have a teammate whom you look up to, or don't think is qualified enough to critique your game, then expand the search to your opponents if you have to.

Okay, so a rival might find it a little strange that you would approach him for advice, but when all said and done, most soccer players are a good bunch of blokes and usually more than happy to help out their fellows.

So try not to be backwards at coming forward, and you should get some valid, well-reasoned opinions and useful tips on how to improve your own scoring, even from an adversary!

Remember, you have absolutely nothing to lose and everything to gain by requesting help and advice from a better, more experienced player, so don't be afraid to ask, even from members of a rival team.

To summarize this chapter: Those who are too afraid to ask are the ones that will never learn or improve.

39 ACROBATIC SKILLS

Being acrobatic can help you score goals that you would never have scored if you weren't so energetic and flexible. Players who are highly athletic certainly stand out from the pack that's for sure.

One of the best examples on how acrobatic skills can work miracles for goal scoring, is to study the Swedish superstar Zlatan Ibrahimovic.

Ibrahimovic is a classic example of what can be achieved when you have exceptional acrobatic skills, as his goal against Italy in Euro 2004 illustrates.

In this game he leapt so high into the air that the keeper had absolutely zero chance of reaching the ball.

I have worked hard to improve my own acrobatic skills over the years. In the beginning, I thought I'd have to visit a medic because of all pain I got from trying.

Learning how to perform skills like the bicycle kick and flying volley, is definitely not something that the faint-hearted should attempt.

I eventually mastered these skills and began to score goals with them, but it wasn't easy and took quite some considerable time.

That said, we all learn in different ways and at different paces, and just because it took me a good while to grasp these moves that doesn't necessary mean it will take you a long time to master them.

One of the quickest ways to acquire acrobatic skills is to partake in some form of martial sport like taekwondo (a Korean martial art similar to karate) or Capoeira (a Brazilian martial art that combines elements of dance and acrobatics).

Zlatan Ibrahimovic actually has a black belt in taekwondo which he manages to incorporate into his game with striking success.

By practicing some kind of martial sport you get to significantly improve your acrobatic skills, and this in turn helps you score more goals.

The reason for this is simple: you become able to reach balls that you would never have been capable of getting to if you hadn't developed those acrobatic skills.

It's best to view goal scoring as something that is pieced together by a variety of skills.

Each skill has its place and comes into its own when certain situations call for it.

The more goal scoring skills you can develop, the more goals you will score, and acrobatics is just one more valuable tool to add to your arsenal of existing abilities.

We all have our strengths and weaknesses, and the sooner you can get to know what these are, the faster you will be able to develop your game.

It is up to you to decide how many goals you want to score, and at what level of competition you want to reach. Just know that great goal scorers are an asset to any soccer team.

The more goal-scoring skills you master, the closer you will get to your primary destination, which for some of you reading here, is to play soccer at the professional level.

40 HAVING A NOSE FOR THE GOAL

You have most probably heard the phrase: "This player has a real nose for the goal" and wondered how he got to score with such sustained regularity.

Having a "nose for the goal" is a skill that cannot be learned from a book, a video, or a personal coach.

This is something that can only come from firsthand experience, and that means plenty of games and lots of goals.

I once got to play alongside someone who had a really great nose for the goal.

It was almost as if he had some extraordinary hidden ability to score the most amazing goals.

Whenever he wanted the ball it would just come to him, or so it seemed, like he was controlling it by some psychic power.

But this was no superhuman with psychic powers, obviously, and his ability was developed over time with hard work and pure determination, as is the case with all the great goal scorers.

He told me that in order to develop a real nose for the goal you must always try to be as near to the ball as often as possible.

He said that it's central for the body and mind to be in balance as well. He also stressed the importance of learning to trust your instincts and going with your gut feeling.

This may have been simple advice, obvious even, but it wasn't something I had given too much thought about until then.

Anyway, I took his advice seriously and on that day something was triggered within me.

All I know is that I became hungrier and more confident for success overnight and have stayed that way ever since.

I want you to remember that you must always, and I really do mean "always," monitor the field for scoring opportunities.

Do this even when the ball is nowhere near the opponent's penalty area.

This is how a true goal scorer thinks, and you must do the same if you want to chalk up a lot of goals over time.

When most of us start out playing soccer, we rarely look strategically for ways to score.

That's because we're usually too busy running around like lost chickens, fantasizing more about scoring a goal than actually doing anything about it.

Having a casual mindset does nothing to help a player improve.

Those serious about self-improvement soon get to see the error of their ways and begin changing their approach.

Developing a real nose for the goal means that a player has to get involved in every aspect of the game and learn how to read the various situations.

One of the key objectives of this book is for you to learn from my mistakes so that you don't have to go through the same setbacks as I did.

From now on, try looking for scoring opportunities with aggressive enthusiasm.

It's time to become that ravenous hound chasing a juicy beef steak!

I can assure you that if you embrace the "hungry dog chasing the beef steak" approach, then you will naturally develop a nose for the goal and become that true goal scoring machine you have always wanted to be.

41 RUNNING INTO FREE SPACE

There are a lot of players who rarely run into free space because they believe the ball will never reach them, and therefore their efforts would be wasted.

Others don't run into free space because they are naturally lazy and prefer to conserve energy for those times when the ball finds its way over to their feet.

If you can identify yourself in any of the above, then I strongly advise you to change your approach immediately. The reasons will become obvious as you continue to read this chapter.

Remember, in a typical game of soccer you will probably have the ball at your feet for about two minutes per game.

That means you will spend most of the time running around without even touching the ball.

So, instead of being idle, or generally ineffective, you could perform runs into free space whenever opportunities allow it.

Believe me, this is a great way to create some ideal scoring opportunities for yourself.

I know how effective this can be because I have scored a lot of goals in my time by running into free spaces.

In fact, this very tactic has been one of my main goal scoring strengths.

Even though I've never been a particularly fast runner, I have always managed to gain a healthy distance between me and my opponents by running into free space.

Think about this for a moment. If you perform a run for let's say 20-30 yards, then there's a good chance you will get a clean pass that puts you into a one-on-one duel with the opponent's keeper.

Even if your ball skills are below the average, you are still in a very good position to be able to score.

By running into free space you also force your opponent to run, whether he wants to or not!

This will probably irritate him and wear him out, both of which will negatively impact his game.

This gives you even greater chance of scoring because eventually he will tire and become less effective at marking, thus giving you a clearer shot at the goal.

There is a lot more to scoring goals than just having the ball at your feet.

You can score additional goals more often simply by running into a free space, and continue running into free spaces throughout the game.

Even when you've barely made contact with the ball, keep moving into free space.

Get into the habit of utilizing this strategy and the rewards will come, of that I can guarantee.

42 PATIENCE AND FRUSTRATION

One of the worst things you can do on a soccer field is to lose your cool and become frustrated or agitated whenever you miss a scoring opportunity, or when something else doesn't go your way.

This will not only negatively affect your ability to score goals, but it will also harm your overall performance on the field, thus making you more of a hindrance than a help to the team.

Whenever a player loses his patience and become frustrated, he diminishes his ability to play by up to 50%.

Apparently this is something that has been scientifically proven.

I was not aware of this fact until one day a coach decided I should understand more about how the brain works when it comes under pressure.

He took a pen and told me that I had to listen carefully to what he was about to say as he was only going to explain it once. He started by drawing an illustration of a brain on the whiteboard, and then said:

"Mirsad, here is your brain and it is separated in two parts, right?"

I went along with his teaching method and agreed that it was indeed my brain that he had just drawn, and yes, it was separated into two halves. He then continued:

"Now listen carefully. When you lose your patience on the field - for whatever reason - and get all flustered as a result, what you are actually doing is disconnecting a part of your brain that's necessary for rational decision making and actions."

"Because of this "disconnection," you will most likely miss one scoring opportunity after another, until such a time as you've restored your calm, which probably won't be until long after the game has finished. Get the point?"

And on that note, the lesson ended.

So basically, what he was saying is that there is absolutely nothing to gain by getting agitated over a situation, and everything to lose. So stay calm and don't let other people or events get to you, or you, and your team, will suffer the consequences.

The coach had obviously taken me aside to explain this because he saw that I was letting missed scoring opportunities annoy me and affect the way I played.

He evidently had a point, and I was left with no choice but to change the way I reacted to circumstances.

This was something that I realized was crucial to my development as a player, so I became mindful about the importance of remaining calm no matter what happens on the field.

This was no easy feat, and I couldn't change the way I was in a single day, but I did manage to change for the better over time.

I can tell that my playing improved immensely once I learned how to react more positively to setbacks.

Not only did I begin to enjoy myself more, but my goal scoring in particular went from strength to strength.

43 BODY LANGUAGE

As you know, good verbal communication is an important part of any soccer game. What you probably don't know, is how the right use of body language can have a positive influence on your goal scoring.

Because of the noise generated from rowdy spectators, it's not obvious that professional players are constantly communicating with each other during a game, yet they are, but not only verbally.

There's an awful lot of non-verbal communication going on between players by way of conscious movements and postures, all of which can be interpreted to mean something specific.

When I first started to play in professional games, I noticed how little I actually communicated by way of voice.

Obviously there's an amount of shouting and short conversations going on in any game, but in the professional leagues there's also a whole lot of body language being read as well, and to great effect.

Whereas some body language is done unconsciously, there are other movements and expressions that are deliberate and require very specific responses.

So long as your fellow team members are able to understand your gestures, then you have a real advantage.

The importance of running into free space (see chapter 41) is a clear example of how body language can improve your chances of scoring.

Once I got to grips with the important role body language plays in soccer, and began to exploit it myself.

It has to be said that I got to see an instant improvement in my overall game, not least my goal scoring.

The more you can read the game, the more you become a part of it, as opposed from apart from it.

If you only rely on verbal communication during games, then I urge you to start learning how to read body signals.

Seriously, this is something that will definitely increase your chances of scoring goals, and it will also allow you to help others to score goals.

Don't forget to use your own body language as well. If this is new to you, then you might want to start by exaggerating your gestures to begin with, just until your team members get comfortable with reading you.

44 SCORING WITH SLIDE TACKLES

While I agree that the slide tackle is not the world's most efficient skill for scoring goals, it can still help you to score goals that you would never have scored otherwise.

I have been using this scoring strategy during my entire career and it works very well when used properly.

Over time, I have learned to score some pretty impressive goals with slide tackles, but the training came at a price.

When I first started to use the slide tackle strategy, I was playing in the position of right fullback.

The negative side is that I caused a lot of penalties in my endeavors to perfect this skill.

These frequent penalties became a bit of an embarrassment for our team, and the coach used to command me not to slide tackle opponents, but his orders fell on deaf ears back then!

Whenever the ball was crossed in from the flank, I would perform a fast run and slide tackle towards the goal. I just couldn't help myself!

The secret to a good slide tackle is to get your foot on the ball without hitting the opponent first.

If you fail to do this then you will get a foul against you and waste a scoring opportunity.

In my time I have squandered a lot of goals by making the mistake of tackling the opponent instead of the ball when inside the penalty box.

This is also a scoring technique that works better during rainy games, or when the field is sodden in places from an earlier downpour.

Obviously you are able to slide several yards further when the ground is slippery, and too far sometimes!

I have scored goals where I have slid all the way to the goal mouth from the 18 yard box.

Only practice and plenty of experience will help you judge speed and conditions when slide tackling in the wet.

Let me give you a word of warning here about artificial surfaces: Avoid slide tackling on synthetic grass at all costs!

You can really get some quite nasty burns from it. I tell you this from personal experience, so believe me when I say that these burns can cause a lot of pain and discomfort.

I only wish someone had forewarned about this the first time I played on synthetic grass!

Try to remember that you should never use the slide tackle as a primary method for scoring goals.

There are times and situations that warrant the slide tackle, but mostly they are uncalled for, so it's best to use them sparingly.

The slide tackle definitely has a place in your scoring arsenal, but don't overdo it.

In most cases it should be your last option, not only because it's the least effective and hardest to control, but it carries with it a higher risk of injury too.

ENDING...

My last advice to you is following: If you have a dream, then do not give it up just because someone says that you will not make it and remember to always believe in yourself no matter what!

25969125R00073

Made in the USA
San Bernardino, CA
16 November 2015